Title: "Game Your Way to Wealth: Mastering Money through Gamification"

By Jenny Koo

Title: "Game Your Way to Wealth: Mastering Money through Gamification"

Introduction

- Brief overview of personal struggles with saving money.

- Introduction to the concept of using psychology and gaming principles to make saving money easier.

Chapter 1: The Psychology of Saving Money

- Explore the psychological barriers to saving money.

- Discuss common misconceptions and mindset shifts needed for successful saving.

Chapter 2: Saving Money Through Gamification

- Compare saving money to video games and how gamification can make saving more enjoyable.

- Discuss RPGs and how they relate to setting financial goals and objectives.

Chapter 3: Setting Clear Financial Goals

- Importance of setting clear financial goals and objectives.

- Strategies for breaking down big financial goals into smaller, manageable tasks.

Chapter 4: Reward Systems and Incentives

- Explore the role of rewards and incentives in motivating saving behavior.

- Compare effective reward systems in video games to those in real life.

Chapter 5: Overcoming Procrastination and Analysis Paralysis

- Strategies for overcoming procrastination and indecision when it comes to saving money.

- Discuss the concept of analysis paralysis and how to avoid it.

Chapter 6: Making Progress Visible

- Importance of tracking and visualizing progress towards financial goals.

- Strategies for making progress visible and celebrating small victories.

Chapter 7: Personal Development and Financial Habits

- Strategies for developing positive financial habits and behaviors.

- Tips for overcoming common challenges and setbacks in saving money.

Conclusion

- Recap of key concepts and strategies discussed in the book.

- Encouragement for readers to implement the tips and techniques learned.

- Invitation to continue the journey towards financial freedom and success.

Appendix

- Additional resources, worksheets, or tools to help readers implement the strategies discussed in the book.

Introduction

Saving money has always been a challenge for many of us. We've all experienced that pang of reluctance when our hard-earned paycheck disappears into the depths of our savings account, seemingly never to be seen again. Despite knowing that saving money is crucial for our financial security and future goals, the act of actually doing it can feel like a daunting task.

In this book, we'll delve into the fascinating world of psychology and gaming principles to uncover strategies that can make saving money not just easier, but even enjoyable. But before we explore these techniques, let's take a moment to reflect on our own personal struggles with saving money.

Personal Struggles with Saving Money

For many people, saving money is fraught with challenges. It might be the temptation to splurge on that fancy gadget or luxurious vacation, or the feeling of deprivation that comes with denying ourselves immediate gratification in favor of long-term financial stability. Perhaps it's the fear of missing out on experiences or opportunities, or simply the lack of discipline and motivation to stick to a savings plan.

Whatever the reasons may be, it's important to acknowledge and understand our own individual struggles with saving money. By recognizing the obstacles that stand in our way, we can begin to address them and develop effective strategies for overcoming them.

Using Psychology and Gaming Principles

Now, let's shift our focus to the concept of using psychology and gaming principles to make saving money easier. At first glance, the idea of applying principles from the world of psychology and gaming to personal finance might seem unconventional. However, upon closer examination, we'll discover that these principles can be incredibly powerful tools for changing our saving habits.

Psychology teaches us about the inner workings of the human mind and behavior. By understanding the psychological factors that influence our financial decisions, such as cognitive biases, emotional triggers, and social influences, we can identify ways to harness these factors in our favor and make saving money a more natural and effortless process.

Similarly, gaming principles, such as goal-setting, progress tracking, rewards, and incentives, can provide us with a framework for gamifying the saving experience. By turning saving money into a game with clear objectives, tangible rewards, and a sense of accomplishment, we can tap into our innate desire for challenge, achievement, and mastery to motivate us to save more effectively.

In the chapters that follow, we'll explore these concepts in more detail, uncovering practical strategies and techniques that you can apply to your own financial journey. Whether you're a seasoned saver looking to level up your savings game or a novice seeking guidance on how to get started, this book has something for everyone.

So let's embark on this journey together and discover how we can trick our brains into saving money effortlessly, one game-changing principle at a time.

Chapter 1: The Psychology of Saving Money

Understanding the psychology behind saving money is essential for anyone looking to improve their financial habits. In this chapter, we'll delve into the fascinating world of human behavior and its impact on our ability to save effectively. By exploring the psychological barriers that hinder saving and debunking common misconceptions, we'll uncover valuable insights and strategies to help readers develop a healthier relationship with money. Let's begin by examining the psychological barriers to saving money.

Exploring Psychological Barriers to Saving Money

Saving money is not just about practical budgeting and financial discipline; it also involves understanding the psychological factors that influence our behavior towards money. Here, we'll explore some common psychological barriers that often hinder individuals from saving effectively.

Instant Gratification: One significant psychological barrier to saving money is our tendency towards instant gratification. This impulse leads us to prioritize immediate rewards over long-term gains, making it challenging to resist the temptation to spend money on impulse purchases or indulgences. For example, instead of saving for retirement, individuals may choose to splurge on luxury items or experiences that provide instant pleasure. This tendency can derail long-term financial goals and prevent individuals from building substantial savings.

Fear of Missing Out (FOMO): The fear of missing out is another psychological barrier that can sabotage saving efforts. In today's interconnected world, social media and advertising constantly bombard us with images of others living seemingly glamorous and extravagant lifestyles. This can create a sense of inadequacy and pressure to keep up with the perceived spending habits of peers and influencers. As a result, individuals may feel compelled to spend beyond their means to avoid feeling left out or inferior, hindering their ability to save for the future.

Loss Aversion: Loss aversion refers to the psychological tendency to prioritize avoiding losses over acquiring equivalent gains. This cognitive bias can lead individuals to avoid taking risks or making changes to their financial habits, even when it may be beneficial in the long run. For instance, individuals may hesitate to invest in higher-yield but slightly riskier assets because they fear potential losses more than they value potential gains. This aversion to loss can prevent individuals from maximizing their savings and investment potential.

Present Bias: Present bias is the tendency to prioritize immediate rewards over future benefits, often at the expense of long-term goals. Individuals exhibiting present bias may struggle to delay gratification and make sacrifices in the present for the sake of future financial security. This bias can manifest in various ways, such as procrastinating on saving for retirement, neglecting to build an emergency fund, or overspending on non-essential items. Overcoming present bias is crucial for cultivating disciplined saving habits and achieving financial stability in the long term.

Psychological Distance from Future Goals: Another psychological barrier to saving money is the difficulty in connecting present actions with future goals. Many individuals struggle to envision their future financial needs and the importance of saving consistently to achieve those goals. Without a clear understanding of the long-term benefits of saving and investing, individuals may prioritize immediate desires and short-term pleasures over prudent financial planning. Bridging the psychological distance between present actions and future outcomes is essential for motivating individuals to prioritize saving and make informed financial decisions.

By recognizing and understanding these psychological barriers, individuals can develop strategies to overcome them and cultivate healthier saving habits. Through education, self-awareness, and practical techniques, individuals can empower themselves to make more mindful and intentional financial choices, ultimately achieving greater financial security and peace of mind.

Discussing Common Misconceptions and Mindset Shifts for Successful Saving

In addition to understanding psychological barriers, it's crucial to address common misconceptions and cultivate mindset shifts conducive to successful saving. Let's delve into some prevalent misconceptions and the necessary mindset shifts for effective saving:

Misconception: Saving is Only for the Wealthy: One common misconception is that saving is only feasible for those with ample disposable income or substantial wealth. This belief can discourage individuals with modest incomes from prioritizing saving and investing for their future. However, the reality is that anyone, regardless of income level, can start saving by adopting a proactive mindset and committing to regular contributions, no matter how small. Shifting the mindset from "I don't earn enough to save" to "I can start small and gradually increase my savings over time" is essential for building financial resilience and stability.

Misconception: Saving is Restrictive and Depriving: Another misconception is that saving requires sacrificing enjoyment and living a restrictive lifestyle. Many individuals associate saving with deprivation, fearing that they'll miss out on life's pleasures by prioritizing financial security. However, reframing saving as a means to achieve personal goals and financial freedom can shift this perception. By setting clear objectives and aligning saving habits with one's values and aspirations, individuals can view saving as a tool for empowerment rather than restriction. For example, saving for a dream vacation or a down payment on a home can provide tangible rewards and motivate disciplined saving habits.

Mindset Shift: Embracing Delayed Gratification: One crucial mindset shift for successful saving involves embracing delayed gratification. Rather than seeking immediate rewards, individuals must learn to defer instant gratification in favor of long-term financial security. This shift in mindset allows individuals to prioritize future goals and make informed decisions that align with their overarching financial objectives. By recognizing the value of patience and discipline in achieving financial success, individuals can overcome impulsive spending habits and prioritize saving for the future.

Mindset Shift: Adopting a Growth Mindset: Another essential mindset shift is adopting a growth mindset towards saving and financial management. A growth mindset entails believing in one's capacity to learn, grow, and improve over time through effort and persistence. Individuals with a growth mindset approach saving as a journey of continuous learning and improvement, rather than a fixed destination. This mindset encourages resilience in the face of setbacks and challenges, empowering individuals to adapt to changing circumstances and stay committed to their financial goals.

Misconception: Saving is Too Complex or Time-Consuming: Some individuals may avoid saving due to misconceptions about its complexity or perceived time commitment. They may feel overwhelmed by the prospect of navigating investment options, creating budgets, or tracking expenses. However, saving doesn't have to be overly complicated or time-consuming. With the abundance of accessible financial tools, resources, and guidance available today, individuals can streamline their saving efforts and tailor strategies to fit their unique needs and preferences. By seeking reliable information and adopting simple, actionable saving techniques, individuals can overcome these misconceptions and take control of their financial futures.

By addressing these common misconceptions and embracing the necessary mindset shifts, individuals can overcome barriers to saving and embark on a path towards financial well-being. Cultivating a positive saving mindset, coupled with practical strategies and a commitment to long-term goals, can empower individuals to achieve greater financial security and fulfillment.

Chapter 2: Saving Money Through Gamification

In this chapter, we'll explore the concept of gamification as a powerful tool for enhancing saving behaviors. By drawing parallels between saving money and playing video games, we'll uncover how gamification techniques can make the process of saving more enjoyable and rewarding. Additionally, we'll delve into the world of role-playing games (RPGs) and examine how their mechanics and dynamics can be applied to setting and achieving financial goals. Through this exploration, readers will gain insights into leveraging gamification principles to transform their saving habits and embark on a journey towards financial success.

Comparing Saving Money to Video Games: The Power of Gamification

In this section, we'll explore the similarities between saving money and playing video games, highlighting how gamification principles can enhance the saving experience:

Clear Objectives and Progression: Just like in video games, saving money becomes more engaging when individuals have clear objectives and a sense of progression. In games, players strive to complete levels, defeat bosses, and unlock achievements, which provide a sense of accomplishment and motivation to continue. Similarly, setting specific financial goals, such as saving for a vacation or building an emergency fund, gives savers a clear target to work towards. Tracking progress and celebrating milestones along the way mimic the satisfying progression found in gaming.

Rewards and Incentives: Gamification relies on the effective use of rewards and incentives to motivate desired behaviors. In video games, players earn rewards such as points, virtual currency, or power-ups for completing tasks and overcoming challenges. These rewards serve as tangible indicators of progress and provide immediate feedback on performance. Similarly, saving money can incorporate rewards and incentives to reinforce positive saving habits. For example, individuals can set up a reward system where they treat themselves to a small indulgence or experience after reaching a savings milestone. This approach adds an element of excitement and satisfaction to the saving process, making it more enjoyable and sustainable.

Sense of Achievement and Mastery: One of the most compelling aspects of gaming is the sense of achievement and mastery that comes from overcoming obstacles and mastering new skills. In video games, players experience a continuous cycle of challenge, progress, and reward, which keeps them engaged and motivated to improve. Similarly, saving money can provide a similar sense of achievement and mastery as individuals set and achieve financial goals. Whether it's paying off debt, building an investment portfolio, or reaching a savings target, each milestone represents a significant accomplishment on the path to financial success. By framing saving as a skill to be mastered and celebrating each milestone along the way, individuals can maintain motivation and momentum in their saving journey.

Example: Let's say you set a goal to save $1,000 for a new computer. Instead of viewing it as a tedious task, approach it as a quest to conquer. Assign each dollar saved a point value, and track your progress like experience points (XP) in a game. Celebrate each milestone reached, whether it's reaching 25% of your goal or hitting the halfway mark, just like celebrating reaching a new level in a game.

Explanation: Gamification transforms saving money from a mundane activity into an engaging experience by incorporating elements such as progress tracking, rewards, and challenges. By integrating game mechanics into financial management, individuals are more likely to stay motivated and committed to their savings goals.

Real-Life Case Study: Sarah, a recent college graduate, struggled to save money until she adopted a gamified approach. Inspired by her favorite RPG, she created a savings "quest log" with different financial goals as quests. Each time she achieved a milestone, she rewarded herself with a small treat, just like unlocking a new achievement in a game. This gamified approach transformed Sarah's saving habits, turning what was once a daunting task into an enjoyable journey towards financial empowerment.

By leveraging the principles of gamification, individuals can transform the saving experience into an exciting and rewarding adventure. By setting clear objectives, incorporating rewards and incentives, and embracing the sense of achievement and mastery inherent in gaming, savers can enhance their motivation and enjoyment while working towards their financial goals.

The Role of RPGs in Setting Financial Goals and Objectives

In this section, we'll explore how role-playing games (RPGs) provide valuable insights into setting and achieving financial goals:

Structured Progression and Quests: RPGs are renowned for their structured progression systems, where players embark on quests, level up their characters, and acquire new abilities and gear. Similarly, setting financial goals can be likened to embarking on quests in an RPG, with each goal representing a milestone on the journey towards financial success. By breaking down larger financial objectives into smaller, manageable tasks or "quests," individuals can create a roadmap for achieving their goals. This structured approach provides clarity and direction, helping individuals stay focused and motivated as they progress towards financial mastery.

Character Customization and Skill Development: In RPGs, players have the opportunity to customize their characters and develop specific skills and abilities tailored to their playstyle. Similarly, individuals can customize their approach to saving and investing based on their unique financial circumstances, preferences, and goals. Whether it's budgeting, investing, or debt management, individuals can develop and refine their financial skills over time, gradually increasing their proficiency and confidence. Like leveling up a character in an RPG, each financial decision and milestone represents an opportunity for growth and development on the path to financial independence.

Community and Collaboration: Many RPGs feature elements of community and collaboration, where players join forces with allies to overcome challenges and achieve shared objectives. Similarly, individuals can benefit from seeking support and guidance from financial communities, whether online forums, local meetups, or mentorship programs. By surrounding themselves with like-minded individuals and leveraging collective wisdom and experience, individuals can accelerate their progress towards financial goals and navigate complex financial decisions more effectively. Additionally, collaborating with family members, friends, or financial professionals can provide accountability and encouragement, fostering a sense of teamwork and camaraderie in the pursuit of financial success.

Illustration: Financial Quests and Milestones

Imagine your financial goals as quests in an RPG. Each quest has a clear objective, such as saving a certain amount of money, reducing expenses, or increasing income. Just like completing quests in a game yields rewards and advances the storyline, achieving financial milestones brings tangible benefits and moves you closer to your ultimate objectives. By breaking down long-term financial goals into smaller, manageable quests, you can maintain momentum and stay motivated throughout your journey.

Example: Investing for Retirement as an Epic Quest

Consider the quest of investing for retirement, often regarded as one of the most critical financial objectives. Much like an epic quest in an RPG, saving and investing for retirement requires careful planning, resource management, and perseverance. Along the way, you encounter various challenges, such as market fluctuations, economic uncertainties, and unexpected expenses. However, by staying focused on your quest and making consistent progress, you can overcome these obstacles and ultimately achieve financial independence.

Real-Life Case Study: Turning Financial Goals into Quests

Take the story of Alex, who approached his financial goals with the mindset of an RPG player. Instead of viewing saving and investing as mundane tasks, Alex framed them as quests to unlock new opportunities and improve his financial well-being. He set specific objectives, such as building an emergency fund and funding his children's education, and devised strategies to accomplish them. With each milestone reached, Alex felt a sense of accomplishment, much like leveling up his character in a game.

Explanation: Applying RPG Principles to Financial Planning

By applying RPG principles to financial planning, individuals can inject excitement, purpose, and direction into their pursuit of financial goals. Just as RPG players strategize, adapt to challenges, and celebrate victories, individuals can approach their finances with a similar mindset. Whether you're saving for a short-term purchase or planning for long-term financial security, embracing the quest-driven mentality of RPGs can transform your financial journey into a thrilling adventure.

By drawing inspiration from RPGs and applying their principles to financial goal-setting, individuals can embark on an epic quest towards financial mastery. By embracing structured progression, character customization, and the power of community, savers can transform their financial journey into a thrilling adventure filled with growth, achievement, and fulfillment.

Chapter 3: Setting Clear Financial Goals

Before diving into the intricacies of setting clear financial goals, it's essential to understand their significance in shaping our financial futures. Financial goals serve as guiding beacons, providing direction and purpose to our monetary decisions. In this chapter, we'll explore the importance of setting clear financial goals and discuss effective strategies for breaking down daunting objectives into actionable steps. By mastering the art of goal-setting, you'll empower yourself to take control of your finances and pave the way for long-term success.

Importance of Setting Clear Financial Goals and Objectives

Setting clear financial goals and objectives is paramount to achieving financial success and security. Without a roadmap to guide your financial decisions, you may find yourself drifting aimlessly, unsure of where your money is going or how to make progress towards your desired outcomes. Here's why setting clear financial goals is crucial:

Clarity and Focus: Clear financial goals provide clarity and focus, helping you prioritize your spending and saving efforts. When you have a specific target in mind, such as saving for a home or retirement, you can align your financial decisions accordingly. This clarity prevents you from being swayed by impulse purchases or short-term temptations.

Example: Imagine you want to save for a vacation. Without a clear goal, you might spend money impulsively on non-essential items, making it difficult to set aside funds for your trip. However, by setting a specific savings target for your vacation, you can allocate your resources more efficiently and stay focused on your goal.

Motivation and Accountability: Clear financial goals serve as powerful motivators, inspiring you to take action and stay committed to your objectives. When you have a tangible goal to work towards, you're more likely to stay disciplined with your spending and saving habits. Additionally, sharing your goals with others can create a sense of accountability, encouraging you to stay on track and make progress towards your aspirations.

Real-life Case Study: Sarah dreams of purchasing her first home. To achieve this goal, she sets a clear savings target and creates a budget to track her progress. By regularly reviewing her financial goals and sharing them with her partner, Sarah feels motivated to stick to her savings plan and make the necessary sacrifices to achieve homeownership.

Measurable Progress: Clear financial goals provide a benchmark for measuring your progress and success. By breaking down larger objectives into smaller, achievable milestones, you can track your advancement over time and celebrate your accomplishments along the way. This sense of progress reinforces positive financial behaviors and encourages continued efforts towards your goals. Illustration: Consider a goal to pay off credit card debt.

By setting a specific target amount to pay off each month and tracking your payments, you can visualize your progress towards debt freedom. As you make consistent payments and see your balance decrease, you'll feel empowered to continue your debt repayment journey.

In essence, setting clear financial goals and objectives is essential for providing direction, motivation, and accountability in your financial life. By defining your aspirations and creating a plan to achieve them, you lay the foundation for a brighter financial future.

Strategies for Breaking Down Big Financial Goals into Smaller, Manageable Tasks

Breaking down big financial goals into smaller, manageable tasks is a key strategy for turning your aspirations into actionable steps. Here's why it's essential and some effective strategies to achieve it:

Overcoming Overwhelm: Large financial goals can feel overwhelming, leading to procrastination and inaction. Breaking them down into smaller tasks makes them feel more attainable and less daunting, increasing your likelihood of success.
Example: If your goal is to save $10,000 for a home down payment, breaking it down into monthly savings targets of $500 over 20 months makes the goal more manageable and less overwhelming.

Creating Tangible Milestones: Dividing big goals into smaller tasks allows you to create tangible milestones that you can celebrate along the way. Each milestone achieved provides a sense of progress and accomplishment, motivating you to continue pursuing your financial objectives.

Example: If your goal is to pay off $5,000 in credit card debt, setting monthly targets to pay off $500 can serve as milestones. As you reach each $500 milestone, you celebrate your progress and stay motivated to tackle the remaining balance.

Enhancing Focus and Clarity: Breaking down financial goals helps clarify the specific actions you need to take to achieve them. This increased focus enables you to allocate your resources more effectively and identify any potential obstacles or challenges that may arise.

Example: If your goal is to start a retirement savings plan, breaking it down into tasks such as researching investment options, setting up automatic contributions, and reviewing your portfolio regularly provides a clear roadmap for action.

Flexibility and Adaptability: Smaller tasks are easier to adjust and adapt as circumstances change. By breaking down your goals, you can pivot and make necessary adjustments without feeling like you've derailed your entire financial plan.

Example: If unexpected expenses arise that impact your ability to save for a vacation, you can adjust your monthly savings targets or explore alternative ways to reduce costs without sacrificing your long-term goal.

Boosting Momentum: Achieving small tasks builds momentum and confidence, propelling you forward towards your larger financial goals. Each small win reinforces your belief in your ability to succeed, making

it easier to stay committed and motivated.
Example: Successfully completing tasks such as tracking your expenses for a month or negotiating a lower interest rate on a loan boosts your confidence and motivates you to tackle the next step in your financial journey.

In conclusion, breaking down big financial goals into smaller, manageable tasks is a powerful strategy for overcoming overwhelm, creating tangible milestones, enhancing focus, maintaining flexibility, and boosting momentum in your financial journey. By implementing these strategies, you can turn your ambitious goals into achievable action plans and take meaningful steps towards financial success.

Chapter 4: Reward Systems and Incentives

Rewards and incentives play a crucial role in shaping behavior and motivating individuals to take action. In this chapter, we will explore how reward systems can influence saving behavior, drawing parallels between the effective reward systems found in video games and those in real life. By understanding the principles behind these systems, you can harness the power of rewards to enhance your financial habits and achieve your saving goals more effectively.

Explore the Role of Rewards and Incentives in Motivating Saving Behavior

Rewards and incentives are powerful tools that can significantly influence our saving behavior. In psychology, the concept of reinforcement suggests that rewarding desired behaviors increases the likelihood of those behaviors being repeated. When it comes to saving money, rewards act as positive reinforcements that encourage us to continue saving and maintain good financial habits.

Importance:

The importance of rewards and incentives in motivating saving behavior cannot be overstated. They provide immediate gratification for our efforts and serve as tangible reminders of our progress towards financial goals. By associating saving with positive outcomes, such as earning interest or reaching a savings milestone, rewards create a sense of accomplishment and motivation to continue saving.

Illustrations:

Imagine setting a goal to save a certain amount of money each month. To incentivize yourself, you decide that for every $100 saved, you'll treat yourself to a nice dinner or a small shopping spree. As you watch your savings grow, you look forward to the reward awaiting you, which fuels your motivation to save even more.

Examples:

One common example of a reward system in saving is the use of savings challenges or competitions. Individuals or groups set specific savings goals and compete to achieve them within a certain timeframe. The promise of a reward, whether it's a cash prize or a shared experience, motivates participants to save diligently and stay on track with their goals.

Explanation:

The psychological mechanism behind rewards and incentives lies in the brain's reward system, which evolved to reinforce behaviors that promote survival and well-being. When we receive a reward, our brain interprets it as a signal that we have accomplished something valuable, triggering feelings of satisfaction and fulfillment. Over time, this association between saving behavior and positive rewards strengthens, making saving money a more automatic and habitual behavior.

Real-Life Case Study:

Consider the example of a person who decides to save a portion of their monthly income towards a vacation fund. To incentivize themselves, they set up a reward system where they allocate a small portion of their savings towards a "vacation jar." Every time they reach a savings milestone, such as reaching 25% of their target amount, they treat themselves to a small indulgence, like a favorite dessert or a movie night. As they progress towards their savings goal, the anticipation of these rewards motivates them to stick to their saving plan, ultimately leading to the fulfillment of their vacation dream.

In conclusion, rewards and incentives play a vital role in motivating saving behavior by providing immediate gratification, reinforcing positive habits, and fostering a sense of accomplishment. By incorporating effective reward systems into our saving strategies, we can stay motivated, disciplined, and on track towards achieving our financial goals.

Compare Effective Reward Systems in Video Games to Those in Real Life

Effective reward systems play a crucial role in both video games and real life, influencing behavior and motivation in profound ways. While the principles underlying reward systems remain consistent across these domains, there are notable differences in their implementation and impact.

In video games, rewards are meticulously designed to provide instant gratification and reinforce desired behaviors. Game developers use a variety of techniques, such as leveling up, unlocking achievements, and earning virtual currency, to incentivize players and keep them engaged. These rewards are often integrated seamlessly into the gameplay experience, creating a sense of progression and accomplishment.

In contrast, real-life reward systems tend to be more complex and multifaceted. While financial incentives, such as bonuses or discounts, are commonly used to motivate saving behavior, they may not always have the same immediate impact as rewards in video games. Real-life rewards also extend beyond monetary incentives to include intangible benefits, such as personal fulfillment, pride, and autonomy.

Despite these differences, effective reward systems in both video games and real life share several key characteristics. Firstly, they are aligned with specific goals and objectives, providing clear incentives for desired behaviors. Secondly, they offer a sense of progression and achievement, allowing individuals to track their progress and celebrate milestones along the way. Finally, they are tailored to individual preferences and motivations, ensuring that rewards resonate with the individual's values and interests.

Importance:

Comparing effective reward systems in video games to those in real life offers valuable insights into the psychology of motivation and behavior change. By understanding what makes reward systems effective in both contexts, individuals can apply these principles to their own saving strategies and financial goals.

Illustrations and Examples:

In a video game, players are often rewarded with experience points (XP) for completing quests or defeating enemies. As they accumulate XP, they level up their characters and unlock new abilities, providing a clear sense of progression and achievement. Similarly, in real life, individuals can set up a reward system where they earn "experience points" for reaching savings milestones, such as saving a certain amount of money or sticking to a budget for a specified period. These points can then be redeemed for rewards, such as a special treat or a fun activity, creating a tangible incentive for saving behavior.

Explanation:

The effectiveness of reward systems lies in their ability to tap into intrinsic motivations and provide immediate feedback and reinforcement. In video games, rewards are carefully designed to tap into players' desire for mastery, autonomy, and social connection, keeping them engaged and motivated to continue playing. In real life, effective reward systems leverage similar principles, offering incentives that align with individuals' values, goals, and aspirations.

Real-Life Case Study:

Consider the example of a company that implements a wellness program to encourage employees to adopt healthy lifestyle habits. As part of the program, employees earn points for completing wellness activities, such as exercising regularly, eating nutritious meals, or participating in stress-relief activities. These points can then be redeemed for rewards, such as gym memberships, healthy snacks, or even extra vacation days. By aligning rewards with employees' wellness goals and providing tangible incentives for healthy behavior, the company fosters a culture of well-being and productivity.

In summary, while there are differences in the implementation of reward systems in video games and real life, the underlying principles of motivation and behavior change remain consistent across both domains. By comparing and understanding effective reward systems in these contexts, individuals can design tailored incentive structures that maximize motivation and support their financial goals and objectives.

Chapter 5: Overcoming Procrastination and Analysis Paralysis

Procrastination and analysis paralysis can be significant barriers to effective financial management. In this chapter, we will explore strategies to overcome these challenges and take proactive steps towards achieving your savings goals. By understanding the root causes of procrastination and analysis paralysis, we can develop practical techniques to address them and make progress towards financial success.

Strategies for Overcoming Procrastination and Indecision When it Comes to Saving Money

Procrastination and indecision are common obstacles that can hinder our ability to save money effectively. To combat these challenges, it's essential to employ practical strategies that promote action and decisiveness. One effective approach is to set clear, achievable goals with specific deadlines. By breaking down larger savings objectives into smaller, manageable tasks, individuals can create a roadmap for success and reduce the likelihood of procrastination.

Another helpful strategy is to establish a routine or schedule for saving money. By incorporating regular savings contributions into one's daily or weekly routine, individuals can develop consistency and discipline in their financial habits. Additionally, automating savings transfers or payments can help overcome procrastination by removing the need for manual intervention.

Furthermore, it's crucial to identify and address any underlying factors contributing to procrastination or indecision. This may involve examining personal beliefs or attitudes towards money, seeking support from friends or family, or consulting with a financial advisor for guidance. By understanding the root causes of procrastination, individuals can develop targeted strategies to overcome it and stay on track towards their savings goals.

Illustration: Imagine a scenario where an individual struggles to save money due to procrastination. Instead of putting off savings contributions indefinitely, they implement a strategy of setting weekly savings targets and automating transfers from their paycheck. Over time, they develop a consistent saving habit and achieve their financial objectives.

Example: Sarah has always wanted to start saving for a vacation but finds herself procrastinating whenever she tries to set aside money. To overcome this challenge, she decides to break down her savings goal into smaller, weekly targets. She sets up automatic transfers from her checking account to her savings account every payday, ensuring that she consistently contributes towards her vacation fund. As a result, Sarah feels more motivated and in control of her finances, ultimately reaching her savings goal ahead of schedule.

Explanation: Procrastination often stems from feelings of overwhelm or uncertainty about where to start. By breaking down savings goals into smaller, manageable tasks and establishing a routine for saving, individuals can overcome these barriers and take concrete steps towards financial success. Additionally, automating savings contributions can help mitigate the impact of procrastination by removing the need for ongoing decision-making.

Real-Life Case Study: James struggled with procrastination when it came to saving for retirement. Despite knowing the importance of long-term financial planning, he often found himself delaying contributions to his retirement accounts. To address this challenge, James sought advice from a financial planner who helped him develop a personalized savings strategy. By setting specific savings targets and automating contributions from his paycheck, James was able to overcome his procrastination tendencies and build a secure financial future for himself and his family.

The Concept of Analysis Paralysis and How to Avoid It

Analysis paralysis occurs when individuals become overwhelmed by the abundance of choices and information available, leading to indecision and inaction. In the context of saving money, analysis paralysis can prevent individuals from making informed financial decisions and taking necessary steps towards their goals. To overcome this phenomenon, it's essential to understand its causes and employ effective strategies to avoid it.

One common cause of analysis paralysis is information overload. With the proliferation of financial advice and resources available, individuals may find themselves inundated with conflicting information, making it challenging to determine the best course of action. To mitigate this, it's crucial to filter and prioritize information, focusing on reputable sources and seeking guidance from trusted financial professionals.

Another contributing factor to analysis paralysis is fear of making the wrong decision. Individuals may become paralyzed by the fear of making a mistake or experiencing negative consequences, leading them to delay action indefinitely. To address this fear, it's important to adopt a growth mindset and embrace failure as a natural part of the learning process. By reframing mistakes as opportunities for growth and learning, individuals can overcome the fear of failure and take decisive action towards their financial goals.

Furthermore, perfectionism can exacerbate analysis paralysis by setting unrealistic standards and expectations. Individuals may delay making decisions until they feel confident that they have explored every possible option and identified the perfect solution. However, this quest for perfection can be counterproductive, as it often leads to inaction and missed opportunities. Instead, it's important to recognize that no decision is ever perfect and that taking imperfect action is better than taking no action at all.

To avoid analysis paralysis, individuals can employ several effective strategies. One approach is to set clear decision-making criteria and deadlines, allowing them to make informed choices within a defined timeframe. Additionally, practicing mindfulness and staying present can help individuals focus on the task at hand and avoid becoming overwhelmed by hypothetical scenarios or future outcomes. Finally, seeking support from mentors, peers, or advisors can provide valuable perspective and guidance, helping individuals navigate complex decisions with confidence.

By understanding the concept of analysis paralysis and implementing these strategies, individuals can overcome indecision and take decisive action towards their financial goals, ultimately achieving greater clarity, confidence, and success in managing their finances.

Chapter 6: Making Progress Visible

Before diving into the sections of Chapter 6, it's crucial to recognize the significance of tracking and visualizing progress when it comes to achieving financial goals. Making progress visible not only provides individuals with a sense of accomplishment but also serves as a motivational tool to stay focused and committed to their objectives. In this chapter, we will explore the importance of tracking financial progress and discuss effective strategies for making achievements tangible and celebrating milestones along the way. Let's delve into the details of how tracking progress can propel individuals towards financial success.

Importance of tracking and visualizing progress towards financial goals.

The importance of tracking and visualizing progress towards financial goals cannot be overstated. Firstly, it provides clarity and direction by helping individuals understand where they currently stand in relation to their goals. By regularly tracking their financial progress, individuals can identify areas of improvement and adjust their strategies accordingly. This process also instills a sense of accountability, as individuals are more likely to stay committed to their goals when they can clearly see their progress over time.

Moreover, tracking progress serves as a source of motivation and encouragement. Seeing tangible evidence of their accomplishments, even if they are small, can boost individuals' confidence and inspire them to continue working towards their goals. It provides a sense of momentum, as each step forward brings them closer to their ultimate objectives.

Visualizing progress also enhances goal-setting and planning. When individuals can see how their actions are contributing to their overall progress, they can make more informed decisions about where to allocate their resources and efforts. It helps them prioritize tasks and stay focused on what matters most.

To illustrate, consider a person who is saving for a down payment on a house. By tracking their savings over time, they can see how each contribution adds up and brings them closer to their goal. This visual representation of progress can motivate them to stick to their savings plan, even when faced with temptations to overspend.

Additionally, tracking progress allows individuals to celebrate their achievements along the way. Recognizing and celebrating small victories not only provides a sense of satisfaction but also reinforces positive behaviors. It creates a positive feedback loop where success breeds more success, driving individuals to continue striving towards their financial goals.

In summary, tracking and visualizing progress towards financial goals is essential for clarity, motivation, and accountability. It empowers individuals to make informed decisions, stay focused on their objectives, and celebrate their achievements along the way. By incorporating these practices into their financial journey, individuals can increase their chances of success and achieve long-term financial stability.

Strategies for making progress visible and celebrating small victories.

Strategies for making progress visible and celebrating small victories play a crucial role in maintaining motivation and momentum on the journey towards financial goals. One effective strategy is to establish clear benchmarks or milestones that signify progress along the way. These milestones can be specific financial targets, such as reaching a certain savings amount or paying off a credit card debt. By breaking down larger goals into smaller, manageable milestones, individuals can track their progress more easily and experience a sense of achievement as they reach each milestone.

Another strategy is to utilize visual aids or progress-tracking tools. This could involve creating charts, graphs, or spreadsheets to visually represent financial progress over time. For example, individuals can use a savings tracker to monitor their progress towards a savings goal, updating it regularly to see how close they are to reaching their target. Visual aids provide a clear and tangible representation of progress, making it easier for individuals to stay motivated and focused on their financial objectives.

Furthermore, celebrating small victories along the way is essential for maintaining morale and reinforcing positive financial habits. This could involve rewarding oneself for reaching milestones or achieving specific goals. Celebrations don't have to be extravagant; they can be as simple as treating oneself to a nice dinner or buying a small indulgence. By acknowledging and celebrating their achievements, individuals reinforce the positive behaviors that contributed to their success and encourage themselves to continue making progress.

Real-life case study:

Take the example of Mike, who set a goal to pay off his student loans within five years. To make his progress visible, Mike created a spreadsheet to track his loan balances and payments. Every time he made a payment, he updated the spreadsheet and watched as the balance gradually decreased. Mike also celebrated small victories along the way, such as paying off a particular loan or reaching a certain percentage of his overall goal. These celebrations served as motivation for Mike to continue making extra payments and stay on track towards his ultimate goal of becoming debt-free.

In conclusion, strategies for making progress visible and celebrating small victories are essential components of successful financial management. By establishing clear milestones, utilizing visual aids, and celebrating achievements, individuals can stay motivated, focused, and committed to their financial goals. These strategies provide a sense of accomplishment, reinforce positive behaviors, and ultimately contribute to long-term financial success.

Chapter 7: Personal Development and Financial Habits

Within this chapter, we delve into personal development and financial habits, offering insights and practical tips for cultivating positive behaviors that lead to financial success. From establishing effective money management routines to overcoming common challenges and setbacks, readers will find actionable strategies to enhance their financial well-being and achieve long-term goals. Whether you're seeking to build a solid foundation for financial stability or looking for solutions to overcome saving obstacles, this chapter provides valuable insights for readers of all backgrounds and experience levels.

Strategies for developing positive financial habits and behaviors.

In this section, we'll explore various strategies for developing positive financial habits and behaviors that can lead to long-term financial success. Cultivating these habits is crucial for achieving financial stability and reaching your financial goals. By implementing these strategies, you can effectively manage your finances, build wealth, and secure your financial future. Let's delve into some key approaches:

1. Budgeting: Creating and sticking to a budget is fundamental to good financial management. A budget helps you track your income and expenses, allowing you to allocate funds wisely

and prioritize spending according to your financial goals. By monitoring your spending habits, you can identify areas where you can cut back and save more money for future endeavors.

2. Automating Savings: Setting up automatic transfers from your checking account to your savings account can help you consistently save money without having to think about it. Automating your savings ensures that a portion of your income goes towards your savings goals each month, making it easier to build a financial cushion and work towards your long-term objectives.

3. Setting Realistic Goals: Establishing clear and achievable financial goals is essential for staying motivated and focused on your financial journey. Whether it's saving for a down payment on a house, paying off debt, or building an emergency fund, setting specific, measurable, attainable, relevant, and time-bound (SMART) goals provides a roadmap for success.

4. Practicing Discipline: Developing discipline in your spending habits is crucial for maintaining financial stability. Avoiding impulse purchases, sticking to your budget, and resisting the temptation to overspend are key components of financial discipline. By exercising self-control and making mindful decisions with your money, you can avoid unnecessary debt and build wealth over time.

5. Educating Yourself: Continuously learning about personal finance and investment strategies empowers you to make informed decisions about your money. Take advantage of resources such as books, online courses, podcasts, and financial advisors to expand your knowledge and improve your financial literacy. The more you understand about managing money, the better equipped you'll be to navigate the complexities of the financial world.

6. Seeking Support: Surrounding yourself with a supportive network of friends, family, or financial mentors can provide encouragement, accountability, and valuable guidance on your financial journey. Whether it's seeking advice on investment opportunities or discussing strategies for overcoming financial challenges, having a strong support system can help you stay motivated and on track towards achieving your financial goals.

Illustration: Consider the analogy of building a house – just as a strong foundation is essential for a sturdy structure, positive financial habits form the foundation for long-term financial success.

Example: Sarah decides to create a monthly budget to better manage her finances. She identifies her fixed expenses, such as rent and utilities, and allocates a portion of her income towards savings and debt repayment. By tracking her spending and adhering to her budget, Sarah is able to avoid overspending and make progress towards her financial goals.

Explanation: Developing positive financial habits involves adopting behaviors that align with one's financial goals and values. These habits promote responsible money management and empower individuals to make informed financial decisions that support their long-term financial well-being.

Real-life Case Study: John struggled with impulse spending and found it challenging to save money. However, after implementing a budgeting system and practicing mindful spending, he was able to curb his impulsive tendencies and increase his savings significantly. By developing positive financial habits, John achieved greater financial stability and peace of mind.

By incorporating these strategies into your daily routine, you can develop positive financial habits and behaviors that lay the foundation for a secure and prosperous future. Remember that building wealth and achieving financial success is a gradual process that requires patience, discipline, and dedication. With determination and the right mindset, you can take control of your finances and create the life you envision.

Tips for overcoming common challenges and setbacks in saving money.

In this section, we delve into practical tips for overcoming common challenges and setbacks encountered in the process of saving money. Facing challenges is inevitable on the journey to financial stability, but with the right strategies, individuals can navigate these obstacles effectively and stay on track towards their savings goals. One key tip is to establish an emergency fund to cover unexpected expenses, such as car repairs or medical bills, without derailing progress towards long-term savings goals. Additionally, developing resilience and maintaining a positive mindset are crucial for overcoming setbacks and staying motivated during challenging times. Another helpful strategy is seeking support from friends, family, or financial advisors, who can offer guidance, encouragement, and accountability throughout the savings journey. Furthermore, practicing patience and perseverance is essential, as saving money often requires time and discipline. By adopting these tips and strategies, individuals can overcome common challenges and setbacks, ultimately achieving greater financial resilience and success.

Illustration: Think of saving money as climbing a mountain – while the journey may be challenging and fraught with obstacles, reaching the summit brings a sense of accomplishment and fulfillment.

Example: Emily encounters an unexpected expense when her car breaks down, requiring costly repairs. Instead of dipping into her long-term savings, she uses funds from her emergency fund to cover the expense, allowing her to stay on track with her savings goals without derailing her financial progress.

Explanation: Overcoming challenges and setbacks in saving money requires a combination of practical strategies and a resilient mindset. By proactively addressing obstacles and staying focused on long-term goals, individuals can navigate financial challenges with confidence and determination.

Real-life Case Study: James experiences a setback when he loses his job unexpectedly, leading to a temporary loss of income. Despite this setback, James maintains a positive attitude and actively seeks new job opportunities while cutting back on non-essential expenses. With the support of his family and a solid emergency fund in place, James successfully weathers the financial storm and eventually secures a new job, allowing him to resume his savings journey.

By incorporating these tips into their savings strategy, individuals can effectively overcome challenges and setbacks, ultimately achieving greater financial stability and success.

Conclusion

In this concluding section, we reflect on the key concepts and strategies explored throughout this book, which have centered on the psychology of saving money and leveraging gaming principles to make financial management more engaging and effective. As we summarize the main takeaways from our discussions, we also offer encouragement and guidance to readers as they embark on their own journey towards financial freedom and success. By implementing the tips and techniques presented in this book, readers have the opportunity to transform their relationship with money, overcome common obstacles, and achieve their long-term financial goals. With a renewed sense of purpose and determination, let us continue this journey together, armed with the knowledge and strategies to navigate the complexities of personal finance and build a brighter financial future.

Recap of key concepts and strategies discussed in the book.

In this section, we revisit the key concepts and strategies that have been explored throughout the book, highlighting their importance in helping readers achieve their financial goals. One crucial concept we've discussed is the psychology of saving money, which sheds light on the behavioral barriers that often hinder effective saving habits. By understanding these psychological factors, readers can better navigate their own saving journey and develop strategies to overcome common obstacles.

Another essential aspect we've covered is the role of gamification in saving money, drawing parallels between video game mechanics and real-life financial behaviors. By incorporating elements of gamification into their savings approach, readers can make the process more enjoyable and engaging, thereby increasing their motivation and commitment to saving.

Additionally, we've emphasized the significance of setting clear financial goals and objectives, providing readers with strategies for breaking down larger goals into smaller, manageable tasks. This approach not only helps readers stay focused and motivated but also provides a roadmap for tracking progress and celebrating small victories along the way.

Furthermore, we've explored the importance of reward systems and incentives in motivating saving behavior, highlighting the effectiveness of both intrinsic and extrinsic rewards in reinforcing positive financial habits. By leveraging reward systems effectively, readers can create a supportive environment that encourages continued progress and success in their saving endeavors.

Lastly, we've addressed common challenges such as procrastination and analysis paralysis, offering practical strategies for overcoming these obstacles and maintaining momentum towards achieving financial goals. By implementing these strategies, readers can develop resilience and perseverance in the face of setbacks, ultimately positioning themselves for long-term financial success.

Throughout this section, we provide illustrations, examples, and real-life case studies to demonstrate how these concepts and strategies can be applied in various situations. By presenting information in an accessible and relatable manner, we aim to empower readers of all ages and backgrounds to take control of their finances and build a secure financial future.

Encouragement for readers to implement the tips and techniques learned.

In this section, let's give you a little pep talk to keep you motivated and inspired as you dive into applying the tips and techniques you've learned throughout this book. We're rooting for you every step of the way!

First off, let's remind you why you're doing this. By saving money regularly, setting clear financial goals, and adopting positive financial habits, you're not just managing your money better – you're paving the way for a brighter financial future. Picture the peace of mind that comes with financial security and the freedom to pursue your dreams. That's what you're working towards!

Now, we know it can sometimes feel overwhelming, like you're not making progress fast enough. But remember, every small step counts. Even the tiniest efforts to improve your finances add up over time. So start small, and don't underestimate the power of consistency.

And hey, don't forget to celebrate your wins along the way! Whether it's reaching a savings milestone or sticking to your budget for a month, take a moment to pat yourself on the back. Acknowledging your progress will keep you motivated to keep going, even when things get tough.

Speaking of tough times, let's talk about resilience. Financial setbacks are a part of life, but they don't have to derail your progress. Stay focused on your goals, and remember that setbacks are just temporary roadblocks on your journey to success. You've got this!

And hey, if you ever feel like you're going it alone, know that you're not. We're here to support you every step of the way. And there's a whole community of people out there on similar journeys, facing similar challenges, and celebrating similar victories. Reach out for help when you need it, and lean on your support system.

So keep your chin up, stay focused on your goals, and keep taking those small steps forward. You've already taken the first step by picking up this book – now it's time to put what you've learned into action. You've got this, and we're cheering you on all the way!

Invitation to continue the journey towards financial freedom and success.

Alright! In this final section, let's extend a heartfelt invitation for you to continue your journey towards financial freedom and success. You've come a long way, but the adventure doesn't end here – it's just the beginning of an exciting new chapter in your financial story.

Firstly, let's emphasize the importance of staying committed to your financial goals. Remember, Rome wasn't built in a day, and neither is financial security. It's a journey that requires dedication, perseverance, and patience. Keep your eyes on the prize and stay focused on the long-term benefits of your efforts.

Next, let's talk about the power of education and continuous learning. The world of personal finance is vast and ever-evolving, and there's always something new to discover. Stay curious, seek out resources, and never stop educating yourself about money management, investing, and wealth-building strategies.

Now, let's address the importance of adapting and evolving with changing circumstances. Life is unpredictable, and your financial goals may shift over time. Be flexible and willing to adjust your plans as needed, but always keep your overarching vision of financial freedom in mind.

And finally, let's emphasize the value of sharing your knowledge and experiences with others. Pay it forward by helping friends, family, and even strangers on their own financial journeys. By spreading financial literacy and empowerment, you're not just transforming your own life – you're making a positive impact on the lives of others.

So, my friend, as you close the final pages of this book, remember that this is just the beginning of your journey towards financial freedom and success. Embrace the challenges, celebrate the victories, and never lose sight of your ultimate goals. The road ahead may be long and winding, but with determination, perseverance, and a little bit of courage, you have everything you need to create the life of your dreams. So go forth and conquer – the world is yours for the taking!

Appendix

- Additional resources, worksheets, or tools to help readers implement the strategies discussed in the book.

How to Overcome Procrastination: Strategies to Help You Eliminate Your Procrastination Habit: First Edition

https://www.amazon.com/dp/B0BQ99KH9V

How to Overcome Procrastination

Strategies to Help You Eliminate Your Procrastination Habit

By Jenny Koo

How to Overcome Procrastination: Strategies to Help You Eliminate Your Procrastination Habit: First Edition

Smart Money Moves: 20 Frugal Habits for a Richer Life: "Small Changes, Big Impact: Transform Your Finances, Transform Your Life."

https://www.amazon.com/dp/B0CQNVF59P

Smart Money Moves: 20 Frugal Habits for a Richer Life: "Small Changes, Big Impact: Transform Your Finances, Transform Your Life."

Simplify Your Life: 50 Rules for Personal Growth, Financial Freedom, and Self-Improvement: "Achieve Your Best Life with These 50 Powerful Rules for ... Overcome Life Challenges and Obstacles)

https://www.amazon.com/dp/B0C2SDCQY5

Simplify Your Life: 50 Rules for Personal Growth, Financial Freedom, and Self-Improvement: "Achieve Your Best Life with These 50 Powerful Rules for ... Overcome Life Challenges and Obstacles)

with a low glycemic index to avoid spikes in blood sugar. Examples include whole grains, legumes, and non-starchy vegetables.

3. Lean Proteins:Incorporate lean protein sources like eggs, Greek yogurt, or lean meats. Protein helps increase feelings of fullness and stabilizes blood sugar levels

.4. Healthy Fats:Include sources of healthy fats such as avocados, nuts, seeds, and olive oil. These fats are important for hormone production and can contribute to satiety.

5. Fiber-Rich Foods:Foods high in fiber, like fruits, vegetables, and whole grains, can aid in digestion and help regulate blood sugar levels.

6. Limit Processed Sugars and Foods:Minimize the intake of processed sugars and refined carbohydrates, as they can contribute to insulin resistance. Opt for natural sweeteners or limit added sugars.

7. Anti-Inflammatory Foods:Include foods with anti-inflammatory properties, such as fatty fish (rich in omega-3 fatty acids), turmeric, and ginger. Chronic inflammation is associated with PCOS, and these foods may help reduce inflammation.

8. Hydration:Adequate hydration is essential. Water is the best choice, but herbal teas can also be included. Avoid sugary beverages and excessive caffeine intake.

9. Portion Control:Pay attention to portion sizes to manage calorie intake. Maintaining a healthy weight is important for managing PCOS symptoms.

www.ingramcontent.com/pod-product-compliance
Lightning Source LLC
Chambersburg PA
CBHW072256310526
45795CB00012B/1704